Community-Based Broadband Solution: The Benefits of Competition and Choice for Community Development and Highspeed Internet Access

1

Contents

Executive Summary

Affordable, reliable access to high speed broadband is critical to U.S. economic growth and competitiveness. Upgrading to higher-speed broadband lets consumers use the Internet in new ways, increases the productivity of American individuals and businesses, and drives innovation throughout the digital ecosystem. As this report describes, while the private sector has made investments to dramatically expand broadband access in the U.S., challenges still remain. Many markets remain unserved or underserved. Others do not benefit from the kind of competition that drives down costs and improves quality. To help fill the void, hundreds of towns and cities around the country have developed their own locally-owned networks. This report describes the benefits of higher-speed broadband access, the current challenges facing the market, and the benefits of competition – including competition from community broadband networks.

~

Since President Obama took office, the United States has significantly expanded its broadband network and increased access. Investments from the federal government have helped deploy or upgrade more than 78,000 miles of network infrastructure since 2009, and more than 45 million Americans have adopted broadband Internet during the President's time in office. Today, more than 90 percent of Americans can access the Internet on a wired line and 98% by either wired or wireless connection.

Competitive markets have helped drive expansion in telecommunications services as strong infrastructure investments and falling prices have opened up a wide range of new communications products and services. Where there is strong competition in broadband markets today, it drives similar improvements. Unfortunately, competition does not extend into every market and its benefits are not evenly distributed. While the U.S. has an extensive network "backbone" of middle-mile connections (long, intra- or interstate physical fiber or cable network connections) with the capacity to offer high-speed Internet to a large majority of Americans, many consumers lack access to the critical "last-mile" (the last legs of the physical network that connect homes and businesses to the broader system), especially in rural areas. It is these last-mile connections that make higher speeds possible. For example, 94 percent of Americans in urban areas can purchase a 25 Mbps (megabit per second) connection, but only 51 percent of the rural population has access to Internet at that speed.

Competition has also been slow to emerge at higher speeds. Nearly forty percent of American households either cannot purchase a fixed 10 Mbps connection (i.e. a wired, land-based connection), or they must buy it from a single provider. And three out of four Americans do not have a choice between providers for Internet at 25 Mbps, the speed increasingly recognized as a baseline to get the full benefits of Internet access.

Without strong competition, providers can (and do) raise prices, delay investments, and provide sub-par quality of service. When faced with limited or nonexistent alternatives, consumers lack negotiating power and are forced to rely on whatever options are available. In these situations, the role of good public policy can and should be to foster competition and increase consumer choice.

At the federal level, the government has already taken active steps to support broadband, committing billions of dollars to deploy middle-mile and last-mile infrastructure, and to ensure that our public schools and libraries have high speed broadband connections.

But local governments also have an important role to play. As this report details, communities around the country like Chattanooga, TN and Wilson, NC have developed a variety of strategies for building locally-owned broadband networks and promoting higher-speed Internet access. Over the past few years, these municipal networks have emerged as a critical tool for increasing access, encouraging competition, fostering consumer choice, and driving local and regional economic development. Local investments have also spurred the private sector to compete for customers, improving services, increasing broadband adoption, and providing more choice for consumers.

Not all communities, however, have the choice to pursue a local broadband network. 19 states currently have barriers in place limiting community broadband and protecting incumbent providers from competition. President Obama believes that there should be a level playing field for community-based solutions and is announcing today a series of steps that the Administration will be taking to foster consumer and community choice.

Economic Benefits of Broadband

In technical terms, broadband refers to a method of transmitting information using many different frequencies, or bandwidths, allowing a network to carry more data. For most Americans, however, the term broadband simply refers to a fast Internet connection—whether fixed or wireless.

Over time, our perceptions of what constitutes a "fast" Internet connection have changed. As consumer and business uses of the Internet evolve, and new applications become more deeply embedded into everyday life, higher speeds frequently shift from being a luxury to a requirement for many users. For example, beginning in 2000 the Federal government defined "broadband" as any service with a download speed of 200 kilobits per second (kbps) or faster.[1] In 2010, the Federal Communications Commission redefined "basic" broadband service as a connection with speeds of at least 4 megabits per second (Mbps) downstream – 20 times faster than the 2000 definition – and at least 1 Mbps upstream.[2]

Today, as everyday experiences for tens of millions of Americans suggest, even these speeds are insufficient for some applications, particularly when a connection is shared by several users. In recognition of the growing need for increased bandwidth, the FCC is considering further revisions to the definition of broadband, and has expressed interest in raising the threshold to 10 or even 25 Mbps downstream and from 1 Mbps to 3 Mbps upstream.[3] The following chart provides a sense of what these definitions mean by showing how long it would take a single user to upload or download different types of content at various connection speeds.

Time Required for Selected Internet-Based Activities at Different Speeds

	3 Minute Song 5 MB (Download)	2 Hour Movie 5 GB (Download)	20 Photographs 40 MB (Upload)	5 Minute Video 200 MB (Upload)
256 Kbps, 256 Kbps 2000 Broadband	2m36s	43h24m	20m50s	1h44m
4 Mbps, 1 Mbps 2010 Broadband	10s	2h46m	5m20s	26m40
25 Mbps, 3 Mbps Advanced Broadband	1.6s	26m40s	1m46s	8m53s

Source: CEA Calculations *Note:* These numbers assume that the ISP is meeting its advertised speed. Download times may be greater during periods of peak traffic.

Demand for Internet access is growing quickly. Total wired and wireless Internet access revenues in 2013 were $140 billion, and have increased by about 15 percent per year in real terms since 2005. [4] The rapidly growing demand for bandwidth is driven by new applications of the Internet that effectively require a broadband connection. These applications, which are increasingly central to everyday life for many Americans, include video streaming, which is used for education, entertainment, and communication; teleworking; cloud storage that allows users to store their files on the Internet, share them, and access them from any device; and online games that allow users to interact with one another in a virtual environment.

Economic studies confirm that broadband Internet creates significant value for consumers and makes an important and rapidly growing contribution to GDP. For example, one study of expenditures for Internet access estimates that as of 2006 – before the widespread availability of streaming audio and video – broadband Internet accounted for $28 billion in U.S. GDP. That study also found that broadband created an additional $5 to $7 billion in consumer surplus in 2006, meaning that consumers would have been willing to pay that much more for the service.[5] Another industry-sponsored study from 2009 estimates that broadband creates $32 billion in annual consumer surplus.[6] While these studies estimate consumer surplus by examining price sensitivity, another approach is to examine the amount of time users spend online, leading to estimates of $2,500 to $3,800 in value per-user per-year, which imply total consumer surplus in the hundreds of billions of dollars.

Over the longer term, broadband adoption also fuels a virtuous cycle of Internet innovation. This cycle begins when new applications of the Internet create demand for more bandwidth, resulting in a wave of network-level innovation and infrastructure investment. As more bandwidth becomes available, application-sector innovators find new ways to use that capacity, creating additional demand, leading to another round of network investment, and so on. While it is impossible to know what the next bandwidth-hungry killer application will be — perhaps it will be the "Internet of Things" or immersive virtual reality — both history and economic theory show that this virtuous cycle is a powerful driver of innovation and economic growth.[7]

The recent history of wireless broadband provides a good example of the virtuous cycle of innovation and investment. Industry studies suggest that between 2007 and 2011 mobile applications development grew from almost nothing into a $20 billion industry, creating 311,000 U.S. jobs in the process.[8] This led to increased demand for wireless broadband, so that by 2013 private investment in new wireless infrastructure was $34 billion, more than the investments of the big three auto companies combined.[9]

Challenges in Broadband Access and Adoption

Since the President took office, national broadband availability has increased at all advertised speed levels.[10] Today, about 93 percent of Americans have access to wired broadband speeds of at least 3 Mbps downstream (i.e. broadband that allows a user to download 3 megabits per second), and 99 percent of Americans have access to similarly fast mobile wireless broadband. This increased availability reflects both private and public investment, including the $4 billion invested through the National Telecommunications and Information Administration's (NTIA) Broadband Technology Opportunities Program (BTOP) and $3.5 billion invested through the U.S. Department of Agriculture's (USDA) Rural Utilities Service Broadband Initiative Program (BIP), both part of the American Recovery and Reinvestment Act of 2009, as well as $66 million through USDA's ongoing Community Connect grant program.

Share of US With Access to Various Download Speeds, 2013
Percent of US Population

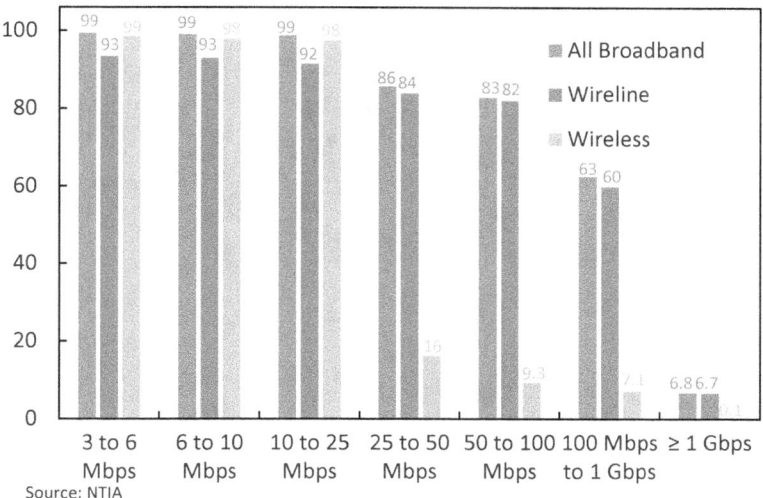

Source: NTIA

Nevertheless, nearly 51 million Americans cannot purchase a wired broadband connection with download speeds of at least 25 Mbps, and only 63 percent have access to speeds of 100 Mbps or more.[11] Moreover, the costs, benefits, and availability of broadband Internet are not evenly distributed. For example, the following two maps show the state-level availability of broadband with download speeds of at least 3 Mbps, and at least 25 Mbps respectively as of June 2013. The first map shows that most Americans have access to "basic" broadband, though some work remains to fully connect the most rural states. However, there is considerable variation in the availability of 25 Mbps connections between states, with some reaching 95 percent penetration and others offering this high-quality service to less than 70 percent of households.

Percentage of Households with Access to Download Speeds of 3 Megabits per Second or Greater, 2013

Source: Department of Commerce, National Telecommunications and Information Administration, National Broadband Map

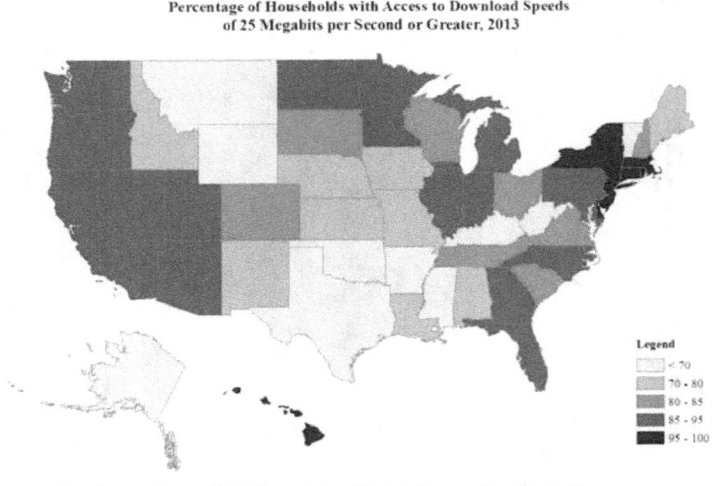

Percentage of Households with Access to Download Speeds
of 25 Megabits per Second or Greater, 2013

Legend
< 70
70 - 80
80 - 85
85 - 95
95 - 100

Source: Department of Commerce, National Telecommunications and Information Administration, National Broadband Map

Urban and Rural Communities

One factor that creates disparities in broadband access and adoption is the divide between urban and rural communities. While the gap for the most basic broadband speeds has almost closed (nearly 100 percent of urban residents have access to speeds of 6 Mbps or greater compared to 95 percent of rural residents), rural communities still enjoy far less access to higher speeds. The following figure illustrates this point:

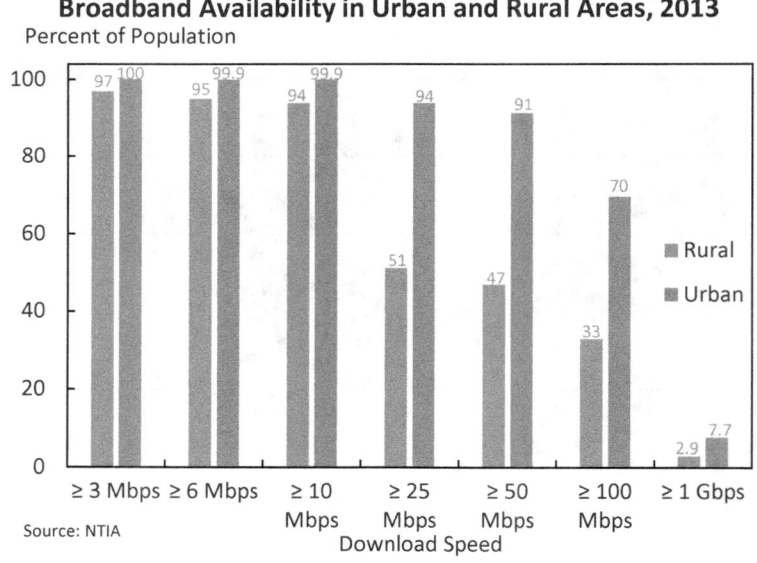

Broadband Availability in Urban and Rural Areas, 2013
Percent of Population

Source: NTIA

The gap in broadband availability between urban and rural communities is linked to the economics of network investment. The costs of providing a connection increase with distance, and the expected profits increase with the number of customers served. This makes it more economical to serve densely populated urban locations, where shorter wires can serve a larger number of potential customers. While satellite and terrestrial wireless technologies continue to deliver promising improvements, more work is needed to close the urban rural gap in broadband availability.

To address this gap, the USDA, BTOP, and the FCC's Connect America Fund program have all invested in creating the middle-mile infrastructure that provides high-speed access to "anchor institutions" such as schools and libraries in many rural communities. With middle-mile and community infrastructure in place, the remaining challenge is to provide last-mile connections so millions of Americans have access to high-speed broadband. As we describe below, the availability of middle-mile connections creates a significant opportunity for municipalities to increase such access.

Affordability

In total, almost 30 percent of American households did not have a home broadband connection as of 2013. One of the main challenges facing increased broadband adoption is price. In a 2010 survey conducted by the FCC, 36 percent of households without a home broadband connection pointed to expense as the major barrier.[12]

Not surprisingly, the cost of broadband represents a greater obstacle for lower-income Americans than middle- and high-income Americans. The NTIA reports that in 2012, 32 percent of families not online with incomes below $25,000 indicated that the high cost of Internet service prevents them from using broadband at home, compared to less than 22 percent of households not online with annual incomes above $50,000.[13] Overall Internet use is strongly correlated with household income, as illustrated in in the figure below, which plots median income against Internet adoption for a sample of 368 Metropolitan Statistical Areas.

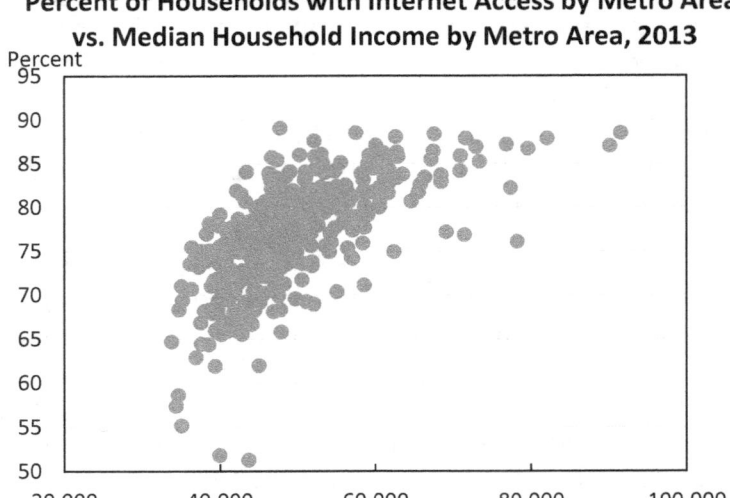

Percent of Households with Internet Access by Metro Area vs. Median Household Income by Metro Area, 2013

Source: Census

U.S. broadband is also relatively expensive when compared internationally. The next chart uses data from a recent report on broadband prices in 24 U.S. and international cities.[14] While the 24 cities in this study may not be representative of all urban locations in the U.S. or abroad, it is notable that the median monthly price at each speed level is higher in the U.S., often by 50 percent or more. And while it appears that the U.S. has less price variability at speeds above 75 Mbps, this observation actually reflects the fact that fewer U.S. cities even offer a consumer plan at that level.

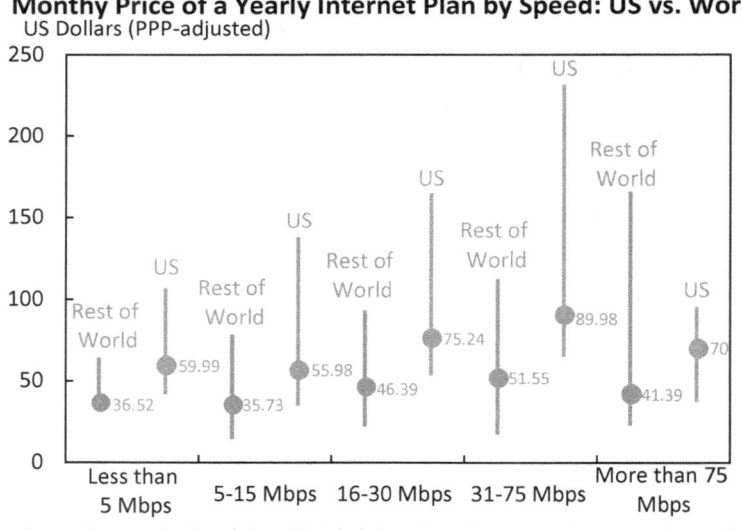

Monthy Price of a Yearly Internet Plan by Speed: US vs. World

Source: New America Foundation, CEA Calculations *Note:* Lines cover price range, point=median

Broadband Competition

One proven mechanism for increasing Internet access, quality and affordability is to promote competitive markets. Over the past 30 years, telecommunications policy has consistently attempted to encourage market competition in local, long-distance and Internet access markets. For example, the threat of satellite services pushed cable companies to expand their network capacity, positioning them to challenge phone companies in the market for home Internet access. And the ongoing competition between phone and cable companies has created a positive cycle of investment, as providers in many communities continuously upgrade their networks and improve their offerings.[15]

However, the overall national investment picture obscures regional variation. Many local and regional markets today do not have the kind of competition required to continue to ensure affordable access to the higher-speed broadband connections that Americans increasingly require. For example, the following table illustrates the number of choices available to American consumers in fixed and mobile broadband markets. When it comes to wired Internet, which can reliably deliver the highest speeds, the majority of Americans have three choices or less. The situation is somewhat better in wireless markets, although focusing on the number of choices obscures the large share of the market served by a handful of the largest providers. And while competition appears reasonably robust if one focuses on combined choices, it is important to recognize that fixed and wireless Internet are not necessarily substitutes, particularly at speeds of 25 Mbps or higher where there is typically no wireless service available.

Broadband Choice for American Consumers

Number of Choices	Share of U.S. Population (%)		
	Fixed	*Mobile*	*Combined*
1	9	0	0
2	33	3	1
3	37	5	2
4	13	22	4
5	3	26	10
6	1	22	18
7	0	11	19
8+	0	12	46

Source: NTIA, CEA Calculations

To illustrate the declining level of competition at higher speeds, the following chart shows the number of wired broadband service providers serving American consumers at different speeds. At speeds of 4 Mbps or less, 75 percent of consumers have a choice between two or more fixed providers, and 15 percent can select among three or more ISPs. However, in the market for Internet service that can deliver 25 Mbps downstream – the speed increasingly recognized as a baseline to get the full benefits of Internet access – three out of four Americans do not have a choice between providers.

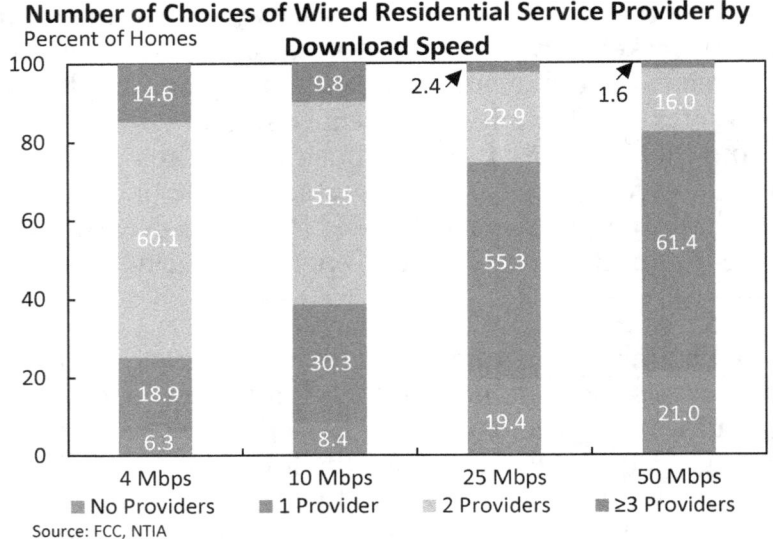

Number of Choices of Wired Residential Service Provider by Download Speed

Source: FCC, NTIA

While increased competition will not necessarily solve all broadband access challenges, basic economics suggests that increased competition leads to a better deal for consumers. For example, a 2014 OECD survey of eleven OECD member countries found that new entrants in wireless markets have a substantial impact on both prices and quality of service. Tellingly, the OECD study indicated that this result occurred even when a market already had three participants – that is, the fourth entrant into a wireless market significantly improved costs and services.[16] As shown above, less than 1 out of 40 American homes has 3 or more choices of providers at speeds in excess of 25 Mbps. Entry also had a positive impact on the market even when the new firm was very small.[17] In the U.S., a 2013 NTIA report found that among those who reported switching their Internet service provider, 38 percent did so to get a better price, and this option is simply unavailable to consumers who are only served by a single Internet Service Provider—or a single provider at the speeds they require.[18]

Even the threat of new competition can lead existing firms to make investments to improve the quality of their goods or services. In the Netherlands, for example, incumbent wireless carriers began offering plans at lower rates in an effort to prevent a new entrant from capturing market share by undercutting existing prices.[19] The U.S. cable television industry also provides an example of the benefits of potential competition. Academic research has shown that during the 2000's U.S. cable television operators were more likely to upgrade their systems to allow two-way communications in cities where the cable operator faced a threat of entry from a local municipal electric utility.[20]

Domestic experiences also show how the threat of competition can produce gains for broadband consumers. When Google announced that Google Fiber was coming to Kansas, speeds on existing networks surged 97 percent—the largest year-over-year jump in bandwidth observed in any state, ever. Likewise, when Google indicated that it would begin offering extremely fast connection speeds in Austin, TX, AT&T responded by announcing its own gigabit network.

Community-Based Broadband

Where the market does not generate the optimal level of competition or investment, the public sector can step in to make investments, encourage competition and provide choice to consumers. For example, government infrastructure investments, such as those made by the Department of Commerce and Department of Agriculture or by Massachusetts (as described below), may be able to put in place the "middle mile" network that lowers costs of entering the "last mile" market. These investments can attract the private sector or provide local governments the opportunity to build their own systems at much lower prices.

Antitrust and telecommunications policies can also promote competition. At the Federal level, the Department of Justice has an important role to play in preventing the unlawful acquisition or abuse of market power. The Telecommunications Act of 1996 also empowers the FCC to regulate service providers in a manner that promotes competition both within and between technology-based platforms such as cable, cellular, satellite, and wireless. The President's recent call for strong Net Neutrality rules to ensure that no company can act as a gatekeeper to Internet content are fundamentally about preserving access and competition in the digital marketplace. And states have an important role in promoting competition and ensuring fairness in their local communications markets.

But these federal and state initiatives are only part of the solution. Local governments also have a critical role to play. In markets where private competition is anemic, whether because of regulatory barriers to entry or the high fixed costs of infrastructure investment, town and cities can build their own middle-mile networks and offer competitive access to the private sector, as Scott County, MN has done. Or municipalities can provide service directly to consumers, like in Chattanooga, TN. In either case, municipalities are creating more choices for consumers, fostering competition and creating opportunities for economic growth. Municipal broadband is often a logical choice for towns and cities that are already served by a municipal electric utility, since infrastructure costs can be shared across those two services, just as private cable companies leveraged their networks to provide Internet service. Hundreds of towns and cities around the country have experimented with these networks and created tremendous benefits for consumers and businesses. APPENDIX 1 includes a full list of municipal networks around the country.

Today, however, there are barriers to community-owned broadband in 19 states around the country. The Obama Administration believes that consumers should have the option to provide themselves broadband services through local government and locally-owned utilities and that state and local policy should support a level playing field for these community-based solutions. This section considers several detailed case studies of municipal broadband initiatives and their benefits for consumers, businesses and communities.

Chattanooga, TN: Gigabit service drives investment, innovation

In 2007, Chattanooga's Electric Power Board (EPB), a municipally-owned utility, announced a 10 year plan to build out a fiber network to serve all of Chattanooga. Based on their analysis, EPB had determined that investments in the network could both drive a smart grid system that would generate significant savings by increasing the reliability of its electricity and also provide customers with improved communication services. In 2009, EPB began offering its triple-play services—Internet, phone, and cable television. Since 2009, EPB has upgraded the mid-tier consumer service from 15 to 30, from 30 to 50, and from 50 to 100 Mbps, without raising costs. In 2010, EPB announced it would offer the first 1 gigabit per second (Gbps) service in the United States. Today, EPB operates 8,000 miles of fiber for 60,000 residential and 4,500 business customers out of a potential 160,000 homes and businesses.

EPB's efforts have encouraged other telecom firms to improve their own service. In 2008, for example, Comcast responded to the threat of EPB's entrance into the market by investing $15 million in the area to launch the Xfinity service – offering the service in Chattanooga before it was available in Atlanta, GA. More recently, Comcast has started offering low-cost introductory offers and gift cards to consumers to incentivize service switching. Despite these improvements, on an equivalent service basis, EPB's costs remain significantly lower.

EPB's investments are reshaping Chattanooga's economic landscape. The gigabit broadband service has helped the City attract a new community of computer engineers, tech entrepreneurs and investors. For example, local entrepreneurs have organized Lamp Post, a venture incubator that provides capital and mentorship to startups. Lamp Post now has over 150 employees in a 31,000 square foot office space in downtown Chattanooga. CO.LAB, a local nonprofit organization, provides shared working space, access to investor networks and hosts the annual summer GITANK program, a 14-week business accelerator. The investment community has responded in kind. Since 2009, Chattanooga has gone from close to zero venture capital to at least five organized funds with investable capital of over $50 million. The growing tech ecosystem has been profiled by the *New York Times*, *Washington Post* and *The Atlantic*.

While the broadband network is opening up new economic pathways, EPB itself remains the most important customer for the fiber network, which it has used to develop one of the nation's leading smart grids. The smart grid, which involves 170,000 intelligent electric meters all reporting every 15 minutes, helps EPB monitor and respond to outages, emergencies, and electricity theft in real time. EPB's smart grid has cut duration of power outages by 60 percent, saving local businesses and industry an estimated $45 to $60 million. With the monitoring system in place, EPB crews can also respond in a targeted fashion during emergencies, helping families and businesses cope with tornados and other natural disasters. [21]

Wilson, NC: Municipal broadband encourages private competition

In November of 2006, Wilson's City council voted unanimously to build a fiber-to-the-home (FTTH) network through the town's electricity provider, Greenlight. The City Council issued $28 million in debt to start construction. Greenlight began offering its services in 2008 and expanded its network to include triple-play (television, phone, and internet) services citywide by January 2009. In 2010, the city took another $4.5 million loan from Wells Fargo to improve its network. The subscription base grew steadily in its first few years and numbers over 7000 today –more than a third of Wilson's 21,000 households.

Greenlight has been a commercial success. Greenlight achieved its first monthly operating profit one year ahead of schedule in October 2010 and made a profit of nearly three-quarters of a million dollars in 2013. However, a 2011 state law prevents municipalities from providing broadband service to other towns outside of its area, limiting further growth.

Greenlight's introduction of its triple-play service has increased industry competition, which has lowered prices for Wilson's residents. From 2007 to 2009, Time Warner raised rates for almost all of its services across the board. According to a December 2009 presentation for the House Select Committee on High Speed Internet Access in Rural and Urban Areas, TWC raised rates in non-competitive areas around Wilson while holding Wilson's rates steady. According to the same report, TWC raised its prices for basic internet service in the North Carolina Research Triangle — as much as 52 percent in Cary — but did not impose any rate hike in Wilson. Moreover, TWC stabilized prices in Wilson for the digital sports and games tier, while Triangle customers paid 41 percent more. The lowered prices in Wilson make a big difference. According to an independent consultant for Wilson, Greenlight saved its residents more than $1 million each year compared to what Time Warner Cable customers in other areas pay.

Increased competition has also yielded increased speeds for Wilson customers. Greenlight's system offers speeds of up to 1 gigabit for consumers and businesses. In 2008, Time Warner's residential Road Runner service in the state offered speeds no higher than 10 Mbps, equivalent to Greenlight's lowest consumer tier. TWC charged $57 per month for the service while Greenlight charged $35. In response, TWC upped its top-tier speed to 15 Mbps "because of the competitive environment," according to a Time Warner spokesperson.[22]

Lafayette, LA: Network increases customer savings, strengthens local anchor institutions

The residents of Lafayette have a long history of supporting local infrastructure initiatives. Recognizing the need to modernize its broadband infrastructure in the early 2000's, the community voted in 2005 to approve construction of a fiber-to-the-home (FTTH) network. After overcoming serious opposition from local broadband service providers, the publicly-owned Lafayette Utilities System (LUS) started connecting homes and businesses to its LUS Fiber network in 2009. The network seeks to provide equitable access to all of Lafayette's citizens, and the system was rolled out across high-income and low-income neighborhoods equally. LUS Fiber now offers 100 Mbps speed for all subscribers.

As competing firms adjusted their plans to account for LUS Fiber's market entry, residents who weren't customers of the network started to see lower prices. Cox Communications, a major regional provider which had raised rates six times in four years, kept its rates stable from 2004 to 2007 to account for LUS's possible market entry. Still, LUS's prices have been consistently lower than those offered by Cox. Terry Huval, the director of LUS, estimates that the community saved $4 million from these deferred rate increases. Using estimates of Cox's average competing discounts and LUS Fiber's lower rates, LUS projects the fiber system will create total savings of between $90 and $100 million over the its first 10 years.

The fiber network has brought in companies eager to obtain fast service at lower prices. Pixel Magic brought 100 to 200 jobs when it built an office in Lafayette to accomplish work on the movie "Secretariat". The high-speed capability of the broadband network was a big factor in their eventual decision to maintain their office in Louisiana permanently. The tech startup firm Skyscraper Holding moved from Los Angeles to Lafayette to obtain 100 Mb/s speeds at a fraction of the cost the company was charged on the west coast. The company pays just $200 a month for more reliable service.

The network has strengthened community anchors as well, delivering greater value and opportunities for connectivity to Lafayette's school and library systems. By mid-2008, all of the schools in the Lafayette Parish School System were able to access 100 Mbps speeds for $390/month. Not only can students now do more to leverage the Internet for better learning opportunities, this monthly fee saves community tax dollars by being a better value than competitors could offer. Lafayette's public libraries also benefit from the network by sharing a 90 Mbps connection from LUS that was rated as the best value amongst possible providers by the federal E-Rate program. [23]

Scott County, MN: Municipal government sees savings for county, school operations

In the early 2000s, Scott County started exploring options for increasing broadband services for county government buildings and schools. In 2007, the County issued $3.5 million in bonds to install a high-speed middle-mile network. The network connects all county-owned facilities, including schools, libraries, city halls, policy and fire departments and public safety towers. It also connects with the state's high capacity backbone network and with multiple private providers. From the beginning, the project was a joint effort between local and state government and the private sector. While the county paid the upfront costs, the state pays for the network's operating costs in exchange for use of the network. The open architecture of the system allows private companies to offer their own services; private providers, in turn, cover the network's maintenance costs.

The network has achieved significant benefits. Scott County's annual bond payment for the construction of the backbone is $35,000 less than what the County was paying for leasing private sector lines. Local schools have seen even greater savings. The costs for Scott County's school districts per megabit of Internet service went from an average of $58.00 to $6.83 per megabit for all school districts—a cost reduction of nearly 90 percent per megabit. The net effect was a tripling of availability (100 to 300 megabits) while costs fell from $5,800 to $2,049 a month. At the state level, the government is saving approximately $1 million per year from access to the public network.

The network has also helped attract significant private investment and fostered job creation. In 2010, for example, Emerson Process Management was finalizing a decision on where to site a new $70 million investment that would create 500 jobs. Emerson's two finalist sites were the town of Shakopee in Scott County, Minnesota and Chihuahua, Mexico. Recognizing the savings from the high-speed broadband network, Emerson chose Scott County. [24]

Leverett, MA: State and federal programs enable local investment

In 2008, Massachusetts Governor Deval Patrick created the Massachusetts Broadband Initiative (MBI). MBI was charged with bringing broadband to all residents and businesses in MA within three years. The Broadband Act provided MBI with initial $40 million in state bond funds. Over the last six years, Massachusetts has built 1,200 miles of new fiber optic cable that provide access to more than 120 communities in Western and North Central Massachusetts.

Of the original state funds, $25 million were directed to build a broadband network in Western, MA. With the support of additional federal funds, MBI developed "MassBroadband 123", a middle-mile network serving 123 communities in the region. MBI worked closely with the private sector to build the project. Today, MassBroadband 123 is operated by Axia NGNetworks. The network has an open architecture that allows any Internet service provider to purchase wholesale services on the network at the same rates. The network also positions municipalities to focus on putting homes and businesses on the network through last-mile connections.

Leverett, MA saw the opportunity to build its own broadband system. In 2012, Leverett voters approved a modest property tax increase and a $3.6 million bond to fund the network. Leverett created a publicly controlled Municipal Light Plant (MLP) entity to own and operate its network, named LeverettNet. The town is currently in the process of building the network – which will provide 1 gigabit service – and connecting it to all 630 households in the community. [25]

Choctaw Nation Tribal Area, OK: Public private collaboration brings broadband to new communities

In early 2009, much of the ten Southeastern Oklahoma counties encompassed by the Choctaw Nation's Tribal Area lacked access to reliable broadband service. The low population density (8.3 to 19.7 people per square mile), the high poverty rate (25 percent of the population below the poverty line) and the rugged terrain made the economics of broadband infrastructure very challenging. Initial capital costs to deploy broadband meant that broadband service was limited only to commercially viable areas.

Pine Tele, the service provider offering voice, video, cell, long distance, and high-speed broadband in SE OK applied for and received 4 American Recovery and Reinvestment awards in 2009 and 2010. One grant was to build out fiber to the home in the area already covered by landlines, and the other three were for wireless – advanced 3G technology – to completely unserved areas. As of September 2014 Pine Tele had deployed 324 miles of fiber, 5,500 fiber drops, and 54 tower sites. New or improved broadband service had been made available to 1,757 fiber customers and 1,194 wireless customers. Today, Pine Telephone provides a variety of broadband packages over both their fiber and wireless facilities ranging from 1.5 Mbps to 5 Mbps for download speeds and 384 Kbps to 5 Mbps for upload speeds.

The benefits for the community have been significant. Every school in the 10 county Pine Tele service area is now connected with high-speed fiber optic broadband service. This has created the ability to integrate online educational tools into everyday teaching and assessments of student comprehension. Broken Bow School District is one example. This district serves approximately 1,280 students per day. They have been able to integrate smart boards, iPads, online lesson plans, and the "I-Ready program" to supplement learning. Hundreds of performance tests are now completed online. And family engagement is improved, as parents are increasingly provided online access to records of attendance, assignments, and test scores. The connectivity also allows the Choctaw Nation to multicast educational videos and share messages from Tribal leadership from a central location. For example, the Choctaw School of Language now offers distance learning courses to approximately 14 head starts and 32 high schools within the Choctaw Nation, in addition to several universities. [26]

Promoting Broadband that Works

Last November, the President outlined his plan to keep the Internet open to new competition and innovation by safeguarding net neutrality — which will help ensure no one company can act as a gatekeeper to digital content. But there is more work to do so that every American has access to a free and open internet. This is particularly true in areas where broadband competition is lacking, resulting in high prices and slow service.

High-speed, low-cost broadband is paving the way for economic revitalization not just in Cedar Falls, but in places like Chattanooga, TN and Lafayette, LA — which have Internet speeds up to 100 times faster than the national average and deliver it at an affordable price. To help more communities achieve these results, support economic growth, and promote a level playing field for all competitors, the Obama Administration is:

- Calling to End Laws that Harm Broadband Service Competition: Laws in 19 states — some specifically written by special interests trying to stifle new competitors — have held back broadband access and, with it, economic opportunity. Today President Obama is announcing a new effort to support local choice in broadband, formally opposing measures that limit the range of options to available to communities to spur expanded local broadband infrastructure, including ownership of networks. As a first step, the Administration is filing a letter with the Federal Communications Commission (FCC) urging it to join this effort by addressing barriers inhibiting local communities from responding to the broadband needs of their citizens.

- Expanding the National Movement of Local Leaders for Better Broadband: As of today, 50 cities representing over 20 million Americans have joined the Next Century Cities coalition, a nonpartisan network pledging to bring fast, community-supported broadband to their towns and cities. They join 37 research universities around the country that formed the Gig.U partnership to bring fast broadband to communities around their campuses. To recognize these remarkable individuals and the partnerships they have built, in June 2015 the White House will host a Community Broadband Summit of mayors and county commissioners from around the nation who are joining this movement for broadband solutions and economic revitalization.

- Announcing a New Initiative to Support Community Broadband Projects: To advance this important work, the Department of Commerce is launching a new initiative, BroadbandUSA, to promote broadband deployment and adoption. Building on expertise gained from overseeing the $4.7 billion Broadband Technology Opportunities Program funded through the Recovery Act, BroadbandUSA will offer online and in-person technical assistance to communities; host a series of regional workshops around the country; and publish guides and tools that provide communities with proven solutions to address problems in broadband infrastructure planning, financing, construction, and operations across many types of business models.

- Unveiling New Grant and Loan Opportunities for Rural Providers: The Department of Agriculture is accepting applications to its Community Connect broadband grant program and will reopen a revamped broadband loan program which offers financing to eligible rural carriers that invest in bringing high-speed broadband to unserved and underserved rural areas.

- Removing Regulatory Barriers and Improving Investment Incentives: The President is calling for the Federal Government to remove all unnecessary regulatory and policy barriers to broadband build-out and competition, and is establishing a new Broadband Opportunity Council of over a dozen government agencies with the singular goal of speeding up broadband deployment and promoting adoptions for our citizens. The Council will also solicit public comment on unnecessary regulatory barriers and opportunities to promote greater coordination with the aim of addressing those within its scope.

Appendix 1: U.S. Municipalities with Broadband Networks[27]

City	State	Name of Network	Type
Ketchikan	AK	KPU Telecommunications	cable
Kotlik	AK	Kotlik	cable
Statewide	AK	Rural Alaska Video E-Health Network (RAVEN)	inet
White Mountain	AK	White Mountain	cable
Opelika	AL	Opelika	fiber
Opp	AL	Opp Cablevision	cable
Scottsboro	AL	Scottsboro EPB	cable
Sylacauga	AL	Sylacauga	cable
Conway	AR	Conway Corporation	cable
Paragould	AR	Paragould Light Water and Cable	cable
Sells	AZ	Tohono O'odham Last-Mile FTTH and Broadband Wireless Network	partial
Anaheim	CA	Anaheim	dark
Anaheim	CA	Anaheim Fiber	inet
Burbank	CA	Burbank Water and Power	partial
Glendale	CA	Glendale	dark
Humboldt County	CA	Digital Redwoods	inet
Loma Linda	CA	Loma Linda	dark
Loma Linda	CA	Loma Linda Connected Community	fiber
Lompoc	CA	City of Lompoc (LompocNet)	inet
Long Beach	CA	Long Beach	dark
Mendocino County	CA	Mendocino Community Network	inet
Palo Alto	CA	Palo Alto Fiber	dark
Pasadena	CA	Pasadena	dark
San Bruno	CA	San Bruno Municipal Cable TV	cable
San Francisco	CA	SF Fiber	question
Santa Clara	CA	Santa Clara	partial
Santa Monica	CA	Santa Monica City Net	partial
Santa Monica	CA	Santa Monica Fiber	partial
Shafter	CA	City of Shafter, California	partial
Truckee	CA	Truckee Donner Public Utility District	dark
Vernon	CA	Vernon Light & Power	fiber
Cortez	CO	Cortez Community Network	partial
Durango	CO	Durango	dark
Glenwood Springs	CO	Glenwood Springs Community Broadband Network (GSCBN)	partial
Longmont	CO	NextLight	fiber

Bristol	CT	Bristol CT	inet
East Hartford	CT	Connecticut Education Network	dark
Manchester	CT	Manchester Wireless	inet
Fort Pierce	FL	FPUAnet Communications	partial
Gainesville	FL	GATOR NET	partial
Hobe Sound	FL	Martin County Dark Fiber	dark
Indiantown	FL	Martin County Dark Fiber	dark
Jacksonville	FL	Jacksonville iNet	inet
Jensen Beach	FL	Martin County Dark Fiber	dark
Jupiter Island	FL	Martin County Dark Fiber	dark
Lakeland	FL	Lakeland	dark
Leesburg	FL	Leesburg	partial
New Smyrna Beach	FL	Utilities Commission, City of New Smyrna Beach	inet
Ocala	FL	Ocala Utility Services	partial
Ocean Breeze Park	FL	Martin County Dark Fiber	dark
Palm Beach County	FL	Palm Beach County	partial
Palm City	FL	Martin County Dark Fiber	dark
Palm Coast	FL	Palm Coast FiberNET	partial
Port Salerno	FL	Martin County Dark Fiber	dark
Quincy	FL	NetQuincy	fiber
Sewall's Point	FL	Martin County Dark Fiber	dark
Stuart	FL	Martin County Dark Fiber	dark
Tallahassee	FL	Tallahassee	dark
Valparaiso	FL	Valparaiso Broadband	cable
Baconton	GA	Community Network Services - Camilla	cable
Baker County	GA	SGRITA Rural Last-mile Infrastructure Project Last-mile	partial
Cairo	GA	Community Network Services - Cairo (Syrup City)	cable
Calhoun	GA	CALNET	partial
Calhoun County	GA	SGRITA Rural Last-mile Infrastructure Project Last-mile	partial
Camilla	GA	Community Network Services - Camilla	cable
Cartersville	GA	Fibercom	partial
Catoosa County	GA	OptiLink	partial
Columbia County	GA	Columbia County Community Broadband Network	partial
Dalton	GA	OptiLink	fiber
Doerun	GA	City of Doerun	cable
Douglasville	GA	Douglas County School System Fiber	inet
Dublin	GA	Dublin	partial

Early County	GA	SGRITA Rural Last-mile Infrastructure Project Last-mile	partial
Elberton	GA	Elberton Utilities	cable
Flintstone	GA	EPB Fiber Optics	fiber
Forsyth	GA	Forsyth Cablenet	cable
LaGrange	GA	LaGrange Telecommunications Department	partial
Miller County	GA	SGRITA Rural Last-mile Infrastructure Project Last-mile	partial
Mitchell County	GA	SGRITA Rural Last-mile Infrastructure Project Last-mile	partial
Monroe	GA	Monroe Utilities Network	cable
Moultrie	GA	Community Network Services - Moultrie	cable
Murray County	GA	OptiLink	partial
Pelham	GA	Community Network Services - Pelham (Pelnet)	cable
Rossville	GA	EPB Fiber Optics	fiber
Sandersville	GA	Sandersville FiberLink	partial
Thomasville	GA	Community Network Services - Thomasville	cable
Tifton	GA	Tifton	dark
Whitfield County	GA	OptiLink	partial
Wildwood	GA	EPB Fiber Optics	fiber
Algona	IA	Algona Municipal Utilities	cable
Alta	IA	Altatec	cable
Bellevue	IA	Bellevue	fiber
Cedar Falls	IA	Cedar Falls Utilities	fiber
Cedar Falls	IA	Cedar Falls Utilities - rural expansion	partial
Coon Rapids	IA	Coon Rapids Municipal Utilities	cable
Grundy Center	IA	Grundy Center Municipal Light & Power	cable
Harlan	IA	Harlan Municipal Utilities	cable
Hartley	IA	The Community Agency	cable
Hawarden	IA	HITEC - Hawarden Integrated Technology, Energy, & Communication	cable
Independence	IA	Independence Light & Power, Telecommunications	cable
Indianola	IA	Indianola	partial
Laurens	IA	Laurens Municipal Power and Communications	cable
Lenox	IA	Lenox	fiber
Manning	IA	Manning Municipal Communication and Television System Utility	cable
Mapleton	IA	Mapleton Communications	cable

Muscatine	IA	MachLink	cable
Osage	IA	Osage Municipal Utilities	cable
Paullina	IA	The Community Agency	cable
Primghar	IA	The Community Agency	cable
Reinbeck	IA	Reinbeck Telecom	cable
Sanborn	IA	The Community Agency	cable
Spencer	IA	Spencer Municipal Utilities	fiber
Webster City	IA	Webster City	dark
Ammon	ID	Ammon	partial
Idaho Falls	ID	Circa	dark
Plummer	ID	Coeur d'Alene Reservation FTTH Project Last-mile Non-remote	partial
Aurora	IL	Onlight Aurora	partial
Aurora	IL	OnLight Aurora	dark
Champaign	IL	Urbana-Champaign Big Broadband UC2B	partial
DeKalb County	IL	DeKalb Advancement of Technology Authority Broadband	partial
Evanston	IL	Evanston	partial
Highland	IL	Highland Communication Services	fiber
LaSalle County	IL	DeKalb Advancement of Technology Authority Broadband	partial
Princeton	IL	Princeton Municipal Utilities	partial
Rochelle	IL	Rochelle Municipal Utilities	partial
Rock Falls	IL	Rock Falls	partial
Urbana	IL	Urbana-Champaign Big Broadband UC2B	partial
Anderson	IN	Anderson Municipal Light and Power	partial
Auburn	IN	Auburn Essential Services	fiber
Lebanon	IN	Lebanon Utilities	cable
Mishawaka	IN	Saint Joe Valley MetroNet	dark
South Bend	IN	Saint Joe Valley MetroNet	dark
Westfield	IN	City of Westfield	partial
Chanute	KS	Chanute	partial
Lenexa	KS	Lenexa Fiber	dark
Ottawa	KS	Ottawa Network	partial
White Cloud	KS	Iowa Tribe of Kansas and Nebraska Fiber-to-the- Premise	partial
Barbourville	KY	Barbourville	cable
Bardstown	KY	Bardstown Cable	cable
Bowling Green	KY	Bowling Green Municipal Utility	partial
Corinth	KY	City of Williamstown	partial
Frankfort	KY	Frankfort Plant Board	cable

Franklin	KY	Franklin Municipal FiberNET	partial
Glasgow	KY	Glasgow Electric Power Board	cable
Grant County	KY	City of Williamstown	partial
Hopkinsville	KY	Energy Net	cable
Monticello	KY	Community Telecom Services	cable
Murray	KY	Murray Electric System	cable
Owen County	KY	City of Williamstown	partial
Owensboro	KY	OMU Online	partial
Paducah	KY	Paducah Power System	partial
Russellville	KY	Russellville EPB SmartNet	fiber
Williamstown	KY	City of Williamstown	cable
Lafayette	LA	Lafayette Utilities System	fiber
Braintree	MA	Braintree Electric Light Department	cable
Chicopee	MA	Chicopee Electric Light	partial
Holyoke	MA	Holyoke Gas & Electric Co.	partial
Leverett	MA	LeverettNet	fiber
Norwood	MA	Norwood Light Broadband	cable
Russell	MA	Russell Municipal Cable	cable
Shrewsbury	MA	Shrewsbury Electric and Cable Operations	cable
South Hadley	MA	Five College Fiber Optic Network	inet
Taunton	MA	Taunton Municipal Lightning Plant	partial
Worcester	MA	Worcester Municipal Fiber Loop	inet
Carroll County	MD	Carroll County Broadband	dark
Columbia	MD	Howard County Fiber Network	dark
Dayton	MD	Howard County Fiber Network	dark
Easton	MD	EastonOnline	cable
Elkridge	MD	Howard County Fiber Network	dark
Ellicot City	MD	Howard County Fiber Network	dark
Fulton	MD	Howard County Fiber Network	dark
Highland	MD	Howard County Fiber Network	dark
Savage	MD	Howard County Fiber Network	dark
Coldwater	MI	CBPU	cable
Crystal Falls	MI	City of Crystal Falls	cable
Holland	MI	Holland Fiber Network	fiber
Negaunee	MI	City of Negaunee Dept. of Public Works	cable
Norway	MI	City of Norway CATV System	cable
Sebewaing	MI	Sebewaing Light & Water	fiber
Wyandotte	MI	Wyandotte	cable
Bagley	MN	Bagley Public Utilities	fiber
Barnesville	MN	Barnesville Municipal Utilities	partial
Belle Plaine	MN	Scott County Fiber Network	dark

Bingham Lake	MN	SMBS - Bingham lake	fiber
Brewster	MN	SMBS - Brewster	fiber
Carver	MN	CarverLink	dark
Chanhassen	MN	CarverLink	dark
Chaska	MN	Chaska.Net	partial
Cologne	MN	CarverLink	dark
Crosslake	MN	Crosslake Communications	fiber
Eagan	MN	Access Eagan	partial
Elko New Market	MN	Scott County Fiber Network	dark
Hamburg	MN	CarverLink	dark
Heron Lake	MN	SMBS - Heron Lake	fiber
Jackson	MN	SMBS - Jackson	fiber
Jordan	MN	Scott County Fiber Network	dark
Lake County	MN	Lake County	partial
Lakefield	MN	SMBS - Lakefield	fiber
Mayer	MN	CarverLink	dark
Monticello	MN	Monticello Fiber Network	fiber
New Germany	MN	CarverLink	dark
New Prague	MN	Scott County Fiber Network	dark
Norwood Young America	MN	CarverLink	dark
Okabena	MN	SMBS - Okabena	fiber
Pine City	MN	Pine City Fiber Optic Backbone	partial
Prior Lake	MN	Scott County Fiber Network	dark
Round Lake	MN	SMBS - Round Lake	fiber
Savage	MN	Scott County Fiber Network	dark
Shakopee	MN	Scott County Fiber Network	dark
Silver Bay	MN	Lake County Fiber Network	partial
St. Louis Park	MN	St. Louis Park	inet
Two Harbors	MN	Lake County Fiber Network	partial
Victoria	MN	CarverLink	dark
Waconia	MN	CarverLink	dark
Watertown	MN	CarverLink	dark
Westbrook	MN	Westbrook Municipal Light & Power	cable
Wilder	MN	SMBS - Wilder	fiber
Windom	MN	Windomnet	fiber
Kahoka	MO	Kahoka	cable
Marshall	MO	Marshall	fiber
North Kansas City	MO	liNKCity	fiber
Poplar Bluff	MO	City of Poplar Bluff Municipal Utilities	cable
Springfield	MO	SpringNet	partial
Collins	MS	Collins Communications	cable

Asheville	NC	ERC Broadband	dark
Chapel Hill	NC	Chapel Hill Fiber Optic Services	inet
Cornelius	NC	MI-Connection	cable
Davidson	NC	MI-Connection	cable
Mooresville	NC	MI-Connection	cable
Morganton	NC	Morganton	cable
Salisbury	NC	Fibrant	fiber
Sylva	NC	BalsamWest FiberNET	partial
Tryon	NC	PANGAEA	partial
Wilson	NC	Greenlight	fiber
South Sioux City	NE	South Sioux City Municipal Network	inet
Cheshire	NH	Fast Roads	dark
Claremont	NH	Fast Roads	dark
Enfield	NH	Fast Roads	partial
Fitzwilliam	NH	Fast Roads	dark
Goshen	NH	Fast Roads	dark
Hanover	NH	Fast Roads	dark
Keene	NH	Fast Roads	dark
Lebanon	NH	Fast Roads	dark
Lyme	NH	Fast Roads	dark
Marlow	NH	Fast Roads	dark
New London	NH	Fast Roads	dark
Newport	NH	Fast Roads	dark
Orford	NH	Fast Roads	dark
Richmond	NH	Fast Roads	dark
Rindge	NH	Fast Roads	partial
Springfield	NH	Fast Roads	dark
Sunapee	NH	Fast Roads	dark
Swanzey	NH	Fast Roads	dark
Glassboro	NJ	Glassboro Municipal Area Network	inet
Vineland	NJ	Vineland Metropolitan Area Network	inet
Churchill	NV	CC Communications	fiber
Bristol Center	NY	Axcess Ontario	dark
Bristol Springs	NY	Axcess Ontario	dark
Canandaigua	NY	Axcess Ontario	dark
Cheshire	NY	Axcess Ontario	dark
Clifton Springs	NY	Axcess Ontario	dark
East Bloomfield	NY	Axcess Ontario	dark
Farmington	NY	Axcess Ontario	dark
Fishers	NY	Axcess Ontario	dark
Geneva	NY	Axcess Ontario	dark

Gorham	NY	Axcess Ontario	dark
Hogansburg	NY	St. Regis Mohawk Tribe Connect (Economic Development for the 21st Century)	partial
Honeoye	NY	Axcess Ontario	dark
Hopewell	NY	Axcess Ontario	dark
Manchester	NY	Axcess Ontario	dark
Naples	NY	Axcess Ontario	dark
New York City	NY	New York City Wireless Network NYCWiN	inet
Phelps	NY	Axcess Ontario	dark
Rushville	NY	Axcess Ontario	dark
Stanley	NY	Axcess Ontario	dark
Victor	NY	Axcess Ontario	dark
West Bloomfield	NY	Axcess Ontario	dark
Akron	OH	OneCommunity	partial
Ashtabula	OH	OneCommunity	partial
Barberton	OH	OneCommunity	partial
Bryan	OH	Bryan Municipal Utilities	cable
Butler County	OH	Butler County	inet
Canton	OH	OneCommunity	partial
Cincinnati	OH	Hamilton County	inet
Cleveland	OH	OneCommunity	partial
Cleveland Heights	OH	OneCommunity	partial
Dover	OH	Dover Technology	dark
Dublin	OH	Dublink+	partial
Eastlake	OH	OneCommunity	partial
Elyria	OH	OneCommunity	partial
Gahanna	OH	Gahanna	inet
Hamilton	OH	Hamilton Miami U	inet
Lorain	OH	OneCommunity	partial
Mayfield Village	OH	OneCommunity - Mayfield Village	partial
Medina County	OH	Medina County	dark
Mentor	OH	OneCommunity	partial
Middletown	OH	Middletown Miami U	inet
New Albany	OH	BlueAlbany	partial
Sandusky	OH	OneCommunity	partial
Wadsworth	OH	City of Wadsworth Electric & Communications Dept.	cable
Wadsworth	OH	OneCommunity	dark
Woodsfield	OH	Woodsfield Municipal Power	cable
Wooster	OH	OneCommunity	partial
Ponca City	OK	Ponca City Technology Services	partial

Sallisaw	OK	DiamondNet	fiber
Ashland	OR	Ashland Fiber Network	cable
Canby	OR	Clackamas Broadband Express	dark
Damascus	OR	Clackamas Broadband Express	dark
Douglas County	OR	Oregon South Central Regional Fiber Consortium Lighting the Fiber Middle-mile Project	partial
Estacada	OR	Clackamas Broadband Express	dark
Eugene	OR	Eugene	dark
Gladstone	OR	Clackamas Broadband Express	dark
Government Camp	OR	Clackamas Broadband Express	dark
Happy Valley	OR	Clackamas Broadband Express	dark
Independence	OR	MINET	fiber
Klamath County	OR	Oregon South Central Regional Fiber Consortium Lighting the Fiber Middle-mile Project	partial
Lane County	OR	Oregon South Central Regional Fiber Consortium Lighting the Fiber Middle-mile Project	partial
Milwaukie	OR	Clackamas Broadband Express	dark
Molalla	OR	Clackamas Broadband Express	dark
Monmouth	OR	MINET	fiber
Mulino	OR	Clackamas Broadband Express	dark
Oregon City	OR	Clackamas Broadband Express	dark
Sandy	OR	SandyNet	partial
Sherwood	OR	Sherwood Fiber	partial
Springfield	OR	Springfield Utility Board	dark
The Dalles	OR	Q-Life Network	partial
Wilsonville	OR	Clackamas Broadband Express	dark
Beaver County	PA	Beaver County Fiber	inet
Kutztown	PA	Hometown Utilicom	fiber
Pitcairn	PA	Pitcairn Power/Community Cable	cable
Hartsville	SC	Hartsville	question
Oconee County	SC	Oconee FOCUS (Fiber Optics Creating Unified Solutions)	partial
Orangeburg County	SC	Orangeburg	partial
Aberdeen	SD	CityNet (Dakota Interconnect)	inet
Beresford	SD	Beresford Municipal Telephone/Cablevision	cable
Brookings	SD	Swiftel	fiber
Bristol	TN	Bristol TN Essential Services	fiber
Chattanooga	TN	EPB Fiber Optics	fiber
Clarksville	TN	Clarksville CDE Lightband	fiber

Columbia	TN	CPWS Broadband	cable
East Ridge	TN	EPB Fiber Optics	fiber
Erwin	TN	Erwin Utilities	partial
Fayetteville	TN	Fayetteville Public Utilities	cable
Jackson	TN	Jackson Energy Authority	fiber
Johnson City	TN	BVU OptiNet	partial
Lookout Mountain	TN	EPB Fiber Optics	fiber
Morristown	TN	FiberNET	fiber
Nashville	TN	NESNet	dark
Pulaski	TN	PES Energize	fiber
Red Bank	TN	EPB Fiber Optics	fiber
Ridgeside	TN	EPB Fiber Optics	fiber
Signal Mountain	TN	EPB Fiber Optics	fiber
Tullahoma	TN	Tullahoma Utilities Board	fiber
Greenville	TX	GEUS	cable
Lindon	UT	Utah Telecommunications Open Infrastructure Agency (UTOPIA)	partial
Brigham City	UT	Utah Telecommunications Open Infrastructure Agency (UTOPIA)	fiber
Centerville	UT	Utah Telecommunications Open Infrastructure Agency (UTOPIA) HQ	fiber
Layton	UT	Utah Telecommunications Open Infrastructure Agency (UTOPIA)	partial
Midvale	UT	Utah Telecommunications Open Infrastructure Agency (UTOPIA)	partial
Murray	UT	Utah Telecommunications Open Infrastructure Agency (UTOPIA)	partial
Orem	UT	Utah Telecommunications Open Infrastructure Agency (UTOPIA)	partial
Payson	UT	Utah Telecommunications Open Infrastructure Agency (UTOPIA)	partial
Perry	UT	Utah Telecommunications Open Infrastructure Agency (UTOPIA)	partial
Spanish Fork	UT	Spanish Fork Community Network	cable
Tremonton	UT	Utah Telecommunications Open Infrastructure Agency (UTOPIA)	fiber
West Valley City	UT	Utah Telecommunications Open Infrastructure Agency (UTOPIA) HQ	partial
Abingdon	VA	BVU OptiNet	fiber
Arlington County	VA	ConnectArlington	dark
Atkins	VA	BVU OptiNet	partial
Bluefield	VA	BVU OptiNet	partial

Bristol	VA	BVU OptiNet	fiber
Castlewood	VA	BVU OptiNet	partial
Cedar Bluff	VA	BVU OptiNet	partial
Chillhowie	VA	BVU OptiNet	partial
Clay Pool Hill	VA	BVU OptiNet	partial
Cleveland	VA	BVU OptiNet	partial
Clinchco	VA	BVU OptiNet	partial
Clintwood	VA	BVU OptiNet	partial
Damascus	VA	BVU OptiNet	partial
Danville	VA	nDanville	partial
Duffield	VA	LENOWISCO Planning District Commission	partial
Eastern Virginia	VA	Eastern Shore of Virginia Broadband Authority	question
Emery-Meadow View	VA	BVU OptiNet	partial
Galax	VA	Wired Road	partial
Glad Spring	VA	BVU OptiNet	partial
Grundy	VA	BVU OptiNet	partial
Haysi	VA	BVU OptiNet	partial
Hiltons	VA	BVU OptiNet	fiber
Honaker	VA	BVU OptiNet	partial
Independence	VA	BVU OptiNet	partial
Lebanon	VA	BVU OptiNet	partial
Luray	VA	Page County Broadband Project	partial
Marion	VA	BVU OptiNet	partial
Martinsville	VA	Martinsville Information Network - MINET	partial
Nelson County	VA	Nelson County Virginia Broadband Project	partial
Page County	VA	Page County Broadband Project	partial
Richlands	VA	BVU OptiNet	partial
Rockbridge County	VA	Connect the Dots: Rockbridge Broadband Initiative	partial
Rural Retreat	VA	BVU OptiNet	partial
Saltville	VA	BVU OptiNet	partial
Shenandoah	VA	Page County Broadband Project	partial
St Paul	VA	BVU OptiNet	partial
Stanley	VA	Page County Broadband Project	partial
Staunton	VA	Staunton	dark
Sugar Grove	VA	BVU OptiNet	partial
Tazewell	VA	BVU OptiNet	partial
Troutdale	VA	BVU OptiNet	partial
Vansant	VA	BVU OptiNet	partial

Wytheville	VA	BVU OptiNet	partial
Barnard	VT	ECFibernet (East Central Vermont Community Fiber Network)	partial
Bethel	VT	ECFibernet (East Central Vermont Community Fiber Network)	partial
Braintree	VT	ECFibernet (East Central Vermont Community Fiber Network)	partial
Brookfield	VT	ECFibernet (East Central Vermont Community Fiber Network)	partial
Hancock	VT	ECFibernet (East Central Vermont Community Fiber Network)	dark
North Randolph	VT	ECFibernet (East Central Vermont Community Fiber Network)	partial
Pomfret	VT	ECFibernet (East Central Vermont Community Fiber Network)	partial
Reading	VT	ECFibernet (East Central Vermont Community Fiber Network)	dark
Rochester	VT	ECFibernet (East Central Vermont Community Fiber Network)	dark
Royalton	VT	ECFibernet (East Central Vermont Community Fiber Network)	partial
Sharon	VT	ECFibernet (East Central Vermont Community Fiber Network)	partial
Stockbridge	VT	ECFibernet (East Central Vermont Community Fiber Network)	dark
Aberdeen	WA	Grays Harbor PUD	partial
Ardenvoir	WA	Chelan PUD	partial
Bauer's Landing	WA	Douglas County Community Network	inet
Benton City	WA	Benton PUD Broadband	partial
Benton County	WA	Benton PUD Broadband	partial
Blewett	WA	Chelan PUD	partial
Bridgeport	WA	Douglas County Community Network	inet
Bridgeport Bar	WA	Douglas County Community Network	inet
Burlington	WA	Mt Vernon Fiber Optic Services	partial
Cashmere	WA	Chelan PUD	fiber
Chelan	WA	Chelan PUD	partial
Chelan County	WA	Chelan PUD	fiber
Cheney	WA	Cheney Fiber Network	partial
Chumstick	WA	Chelan PUD	partial
Clallam County	WA	Clallam PUD	partial
Coulee City	WA	Grant PUD	partial
Coulee Dam	WA	Grant PUD	partial

Desert Aire	WA	Grant PUD	fiber
Desert Canyon	WA	Douglas County Community Network	inet
Douglas County	WA	Douglas County Community Network	inet
Dryden	WA	Chelan PUD	fiber
East Wenatchee	WA	Douglas County Community Network	inet
Edmonds	WA	City of Edmonds	dark
Entiat	WA	Chelan PUD	partial
Ephrata	WA	Grant PUD	partial
Franklin County	WA	Franklin PUD Broadband	partial
Grand Coulee	WA	Grant PUD	fiber
Grant County	WA	Grant PUD	fiber
Hartline	WA	Grant PUD	fiber
Kennewick	WA	Benton PUD Broadband	fiber
Kitsap County	WA	Kitsap PUD	fiber
Leavenworth	WA	Chelan PUD	fiber
Mansfield	WA	Douglas County Community Network	inet
Mason County	WA	Mason County PUD3	partial
Mattawa	WA	Grant PUD	fiber
Meritt	WA	Chelan PUD	partial
Monitor	WA	Chelan PUD	fiber
Moses Lake	WA	Grant PUD	partial
Mt Vernon	WA	Mt Vernon Fiber Optic Services	partial
Newport	WA	Pend Oreille County Public Utility District (PUD) Broadband Network	partial
Okanogan County	WA	Okanogan PUD	fiber
Orondo	WA	Douglas County Community Network	inet
Pacific County	WA	Pacific County PUD#2	partial
Pasco	WA	Franklin PUD Broadband	fiber
Pend Oreille County	WA	Pend Oreille PUD	fiber
Peshastin	WA	Chelan PUD	fiber
Port of Skagit County	WA	Mt Vernon Fiber Optic Services	partial
Prosser	WA	Benton PUD Broadband	fiber
Quincy	WA	Grant PUD	fiber
Royal City	WA	Grant PUD	fiber
Sequim	WA	Clallam PUD	partial
Shelton	WA	Mason County Public Utilities District	partial
Soap Lake	WA	Grant PUD	fiber
Sun Cove	WA	Douglas County Community Network	inet
Tacoma	WA	Click! Network	cable
Warden	WA	Grant PUD	fiber

Waterville	WA	Douglas County Community Network	inet
Wenatchee	WA	Chelan PUD	fiber
Wilson Creek	WA	Grant PUD	fiber
Yodelin	WA	Chelan PUD	partial
Eau Claire	WI	Chippewa Internetworking Consortium (CINC)	inet
Oconto	WI	Oconto Falls Municipal Utilities	cable
Platteville	WI	Chippewa Internetworking Consortium (CINC)	partial
Reedsburg	WI	Reedsburg Utility Commission	fiber
Reedsburg	WI	Reedsburg Utility Commission - rural expansion	partial
Shawano	WI	Shawano Municipal Utilities	fiber
Sun Prairie	WI	Sun Prairie Utilities	partial
Superior	WI	Chippewa Internetworking Consortium (CINC)	partial
Wausau	WI	Chippewa Internetworking Consortium (CINC)	partial
Philippi	WV	Philippi Communications System	fiber
Powell	WY	Powell Fiber Optic Network	fiber

[1] National Telecommunications and Information Administration (NTIA). 2013. "US Broadband Availability: June 2010-June 2012." http://www.ntia.doc.gov/files/ntia/publications/usbb_avail_report_05102013.pdf, 3.

[2] Federal Communications Commission. 2010. "Sixth Broadband Deployment Report." July 20. https://apps.fcc.gov/edocs_public/attachmatch/FCC-10-129A1_Rcd.pdf.

[3] Federal Communications Commission. 2014. "Tenth Broadband Progress Notice of Inquiry." August 5. https://apps.fcc.gov/edocs_public/attachmatch/FCC-14-113A1.pdf

[4] United States Census Bureau. "Table 4: Estimated Sources of Revenue for Employer Firms: 2010 through 2013." November 19. *Annual and Quarterly Services.* https://www.census.gov/services/index.html (CEA Calculations).

[5] Greenstein, Shane and Ryan C. McDevitt. 2009. "The Broadband Bonus: Accounting for Broadband Internet's Impact on U.S. GDP" NBER Working Paper No. 14758. http://www.nber.org/papers/w14758. This study suggests that roughly 50 percent of this amount– $8 to $11 billion– was "new GDP" that would not have been realized but for the replacement of dial-up with broadband connections.

[6] Dutz, Mark, Jonathan Orszag, and Robert Willig. 2009. "The Substantial Consumer Benefits of Broadband Connectivity for U.S. Households." COMPASS LEXECON, commissioned by the Internet Innovation Alliance, July. http://internetinnovation.org/files/special-reports/CONSUMER_BENEFITS_OF_BROADBAND.pdf.

[7] Bresnahan, Timothy F., and Shane Greenstein. 1999. "Technology Competition and the Structure of the Computer Industry." *Journal of Industrial Economics* 47: 1-40, DOI: 10.1111/1467-6451.00088.

[8] Mandel, Dr. Michael. 2012. "Where the Jobs Are: The App Economy." February 2. https://www.conference-board.org/retrievefile.cfm?filename=Where-the-Jobs-Are_-The-App-Economy.pdf&type=subsite.

[9] US Telecom. The Broadband Association. "Broadband Investment." http://www.ustelecom.org/broadband-industry/broadband-industry-stats/investment; Carew, Diana G. and Michael Mandel. 2012. "Investment Heroes: Who's Betting on America's Future?" Progressive Policy Institute, July. http://progressivepolicy.org/wp-content/uploads/2012/07/07.2012-Mandel_Carew_Investment-Heroes_Whos-Betting-on-Americas-Future.pdf.

[10] NTIA, 2013.

[11] Office of Science and Technology Policy & The National Economic Council. 2013. "Four Years of Broadband Growth." June. http://www.whitehouse.gov/sites/default/files/broadband_report_final.pdf.

[12] Horrigan, John B. 2010. "Broadband Adoption & Use in America. Results from an FCC Survey.". March. http://transition.fcc.gov/DiversityFAC/032410/consumer-survey-horrigan.pdf.

[13] Department of Commerce (NTIA and ESA). 2013. "Exploring the Digital Nation. America's Emerging Online Experience." June. http://www.ntia.doc.gov/files/ntia/publications/exploring_the_digital_nation_-_americas_emerging_online_experience.pdf, page 39.

[14] Hibah, Hussain, Danielle Kehl, Patrick Lucey, and Nick Russo. 2013. "The Cost of Connectivity 2013. Data Release: A comparison of high-speed Internet prices in 24 cities around the world." New America Foundation, October. http://oti.newamerica.net/publications/policy/the_cost_of_connectivity_2013. The US cities included are: Bristol (VA), Chattanooga (TN), Kansas City (MO), Lafayette (LA), Los Angeles (CA), New York (NY), San Francisco (CA), and Washington (DC). The international cities included are: Toronto (Canada), Hong Kong, Prague (Czech Republic), Copenhagen (Denmark), Paris (France), Berlin (Germany), Dublin (Ireland), Tokyo (Japan), Riga (Latvia), Mexico City

(Mexico), Amsterdam (Netherlands), Bucharest (Romania), Seoul (South Korea), Zurich (Switzerland), and London (UK). Some of these cities are omitted from the data underlying the chart below, as the plans included in NAF's dataset are not all annual contracts.

[15]Wheeler, Tom. 2014. "Prepared Remarks of Chairman Tom Wheeler. 'The Facts and Future of Broadband Competition.'" September 4. https://apps.fcc.gov/edocs_public/attachmatch/DOC-329161A1.pdf.

[16]OECD. 2014. "Wireless Market Structures and Network Sharing." *OECD Digital Economy Papers,* No. 243. OECD Publishing. http://dx.doi.org/10.1787/5jxt46dzl9r2-en.

[17]The case of 3UK is cited by OECD as particularly indicative of this reality.

[18] Department of Commerce (NTIA and ESA). 2013. "Exploring the Digital Nation. America's Emerging Online Experience." June. http://www.ntia.doc.gov/files/ntia/publications/exploring_the_digital_nation_-_americas_emerging_online_experience.pdf, page 39.

[19] OECD. 2014.

[20]Seamans, Robert. 2012. Fighting City Hall: Entry Deterrence and Technology Deployment in the
Cable TV Industry. *Management Science* 58(3): 461-475.

[21]Sources used to prepare this case study: Technology, Gig, and Entrepreneurship Task Force. 2014. "Chattanooga Forward." March 19. http://www.chattanooga.gov/images/Mayor_Images/Chattanooga_Forward_Working_report.pdf; Wyatt, Edward. 2014. "Fast Internet is Chattanooga's New Locomotive." *New York Times,* February 3. http://www.nytimes.com/2014/02/04/technology/fast-internet-service-speeds-business-development-in-chattanooga.html; Fung, Brian. 2013. "How Chattanooga beat Google Fiber by half a decade." *Washington Post,* September 17. http://www.washingtonpost.com/blogs/the-switch/wp/2013/09/17/how-chattanooga-beat-google-fiber-by-half-a-decade; Rushe, Dominic. 2014. "Chattanooga's Gig: how one city's super-fast internet is driving a tech boom." *The Guardian*, August 30. http://www.theguardian.com/world/2014/aug/30/chattanooga-gig-high-speed-internet-tech-boom; Cosco, Joey. 2014. "A City in Tennessee Has The Big Cable Companies Terrified." *Business Insider,* July 30. http://www.businessinsider.com/chattanooga-tennessee-big-internet-companies-terrified-2014-7; Mitchell, Christopher. 2012. "Broadband At the Speed of Light. How Three Communities Built Next-Generation Networks." April. Institute for Local Self-Reliance and Benton Foundation, April. http://ilsr.org/wp-content/uploads/2012/04/muni-bb-speed-light.pdf.

[22]Sources used to prepare this case study:
Mitchell, Christopher. O'Boyle, Todd. 2012. "Carolina's Connected Community: Wilson Gives Greenlight to Fast Internet." December. Institute for Local Self-Reliance and Common Cause Education Fund, December. http://ilsr.org/wp-content/uploads/2012/12/wilson-greenlight.pdf; New York Times. 2014. "Communities Fight State Laws That Can Divide Broadband Access." November 9. http://www.nytimes.com/2014/11/10/technology/in-rural-america-challenging-a-roadblock-to-high-speed-internet.html; Indy Week. 2008. "Mighty, mighty broadband." June 18. http://www.indyweek.com/indyweek/mighty-mighty-broadband/Content?oid=1209049; Wired.com. 2011. "North Carolina Enacts Pro-ISP, Anti-Municipal Broadband Law." May 23. http://www.wired.com/2011/05/nc-gov-anti-muni-broadband/; Davidson, Charles M. Santorelli, Michael J. 2014. "Understanding The Debate Over Government-owned Broadband Networks: Context, Lessons Learned, and a Way Forward for Policy Makers." June. Advanced Communications Law and Policy Institute at New York Law School, June. http://www.nyls.edu/advanced-communications-law-and-policy-institute/wp-

content/uploads/sites/169/2013/08/ACLP-%E2%80%93-Wilson-Case-Study-%E2%80%93-June-2014.pdf; Wilson Times. 2010. "Greenlight competition affects rates elsewhere." http://www.wilsontimes.com/greenlight/Story/Greenlight-competition-affects-rates-elsewhere
[23]Sources used to prepare this case study:
Huval, Terry. 2010. Testimony Before the Committee on Small Business and Entrepreneurship. *Hearing on "Connecting Main Street to the World: Federal Efforts to Expand Small Business Internet Access."* Senate Hearing 111-1166, April 27. http://www.sbc.senate.gov/public/index.cfm?a=Files.Serve&File_id=646b01b6-6e75-4f5a-9c0f-790c0ba48889
Jervis, Rick. 2012. "Louisiana city blazes high-speed Web trail." *USA Today*, February 5. http://usatoday30.usatoday.com/news/nation/story/2012-02-01/broadband-telecom-lafayette/52920278/1
Mitchell, Christopher. 2012. "Broadband at the Speed of Light: How Three Communities Built Next-Generation Networks." April. Institute for Local Self-Reliance and Benton Foundation, April. http://ilsr.org/wp-content/uploads/2012/04/muni-bb-speed-light.pdf
Pollick, Michael. 2010. "Dark lines are a draw for business". *Sarasota Harold-Tribune*, September 7. http://www.heraldtribune.com/article/20100907/ARTICLE/100909825/-1/news?p=all&tc=pgall
[24]Sources used for this case study: Collaborative Governance Council. 2010. "Scott County Broadband (Fiber) Project." Minnesota Office of the State Auditor, August 12. http://www.osa.state.mn.us/Other/councils/CollaborativeGovernance/081210/ScottCountyBroadbandProjectPresentation.pdf; Minnesota Ultra High Speed Broadband Task Force. 2009. "Scott County Broadband (Fiber) Approach." February 20. http://www.ultra-high-speed-mn.org/CM/Custom/Shelton%20-%20Broadband%20Task%20force%20Presentation.pdf; Moore, Janet. 2013. "Scott County approves incentives for Shutterfly." *Minnesota Star Tribune*, August 20. http://www.startribune.com/blogs/220393971.html; Mitchell, Chris, and Lisa Gonzalez. 2014. "All Hangs on Deck. Minnesota Local Government Models for Expanding Fiber Internet Access." Institute for Local Self-Reliance, September. http://www.ilsr.org/wp-content/uploads/downloads/2014/09/all_hands_on_deck_mn.pdf.

[25]Sources used for this case: Gonzalez, Lisa. 2012. "Network Moves Forward in Leverett, Western Massachusetts." Community Broadband Networks, December 20. http://www.muninetworks.org/content/network-moves-forward-leverett-western-massachusetts; Crawford, Susan and Robyn Mohr. 2013. "Bringing Municipal HighSpeed Internet Access to Leverett, Massachusetts." Harvard University Berkman Center Research Publication No. 26, December 17. http://papers.ssrn.com/sol3/papers.cfm?abstract_id=2366044; Lennett, Benjamin, Patrick Lucey, Joanne Hovis, and Andrew Afflerbach. "The Art of the Possible: An Overview of Public Broadband Options." New American Foundation Open Technology Institute and CTC Technology & Energy, May 6. http://newamerica.net/sites/newamerica.net/files/policydocs/TheArtofthePossibleOverviewofPublicBroadbandOptions_NAFOTI-CTC.pdf; Scherban, Debra. 2014. "Crocker Communications to provide Internet Service for Leverett's own broadband network." *Daily Hampshire Gazette*, September 2. http://www.gazettenet.com/home/13387776-95/crocker-communications-to-provide-internet-service-for-leveretts-own-broadband-network.

[26] Sources used for this case: Yocum, Katie. 2010. "USDA Recovery Act-Funded Wireless Internet to Reach Remote Choctaw Nation." United States Department of Agriculture, June 11. http://blogs.usda.gov/2010/06/11/usda-recovery-act-funded-wireless-Internet-to-reach-remote-choctaw-nation; The Choctaw Nation of Oklahoma. "Programs & Services for the Choctaw People." http://s3.amazonaws.com/choctaw-msldigital/assets/2345/choctaw_services_original.pdf. Material from a site visit conducted by USDA from September 22 to 25, 2014 in Broken Bow, Oklahoma was also relied upon for the Pine Telephone Company Case Study.

[27] The Institute for Local Self-Reliance, data provided to NEC/CEA upon request.

www.ingramcontent.com/pod-product-compliance
Lightning Source LLC
Chambersburg PA
CBHW081134280526
45787CB00007B/3078